SPEEDY
TRAINS

KINGFISHER
LONDON & NEW YORK

KINGFISHER
LONDON & NEW YORK

Copyright © Macmillan Publishers International Ltd 2016, 2021
First published in 2016 in the United States by Kingfisher
This edition published in 2021 by Kingfisher
120 Broadway, New York, NY 10271
Kingfisher is an imprint of Macmillan Children's Books, London

Distributed in the U.S. and Canada by Macmillan,
120 Broadway, New York, NY 10271

Library of Congress Cataloging-in-Publication data has been applied for.

Series editor: Sarah Snashall
Series design: Little Red Ant and Laura Hall
Adapted from an original text by Chris Oxlade and Thea Feldman

ISBN 978-0-7534-7669-7

Kingfisher books are available for special prootions and premiums.
For details contact: Special Markets Department, Macmillan,
120 Broadway, New York, NY 10271.

For more information, please visit www.kingfisherbooks.com

Printed in China
9 8 7 6 5 4 3 2 1
1TR/0221/WKT/UG/128MA

EU representative: Macmillan Publishers Ireland Limited,
Mallard Lodge, Lansdowne Village, Dublin 4

Picture credits
The Publisher would like to thank the following for permission to reproduce
their material.
Top = t; Bottom = b; Center = c; Left = l; Right = r
Cover Shutterstock/topimages; Back cover, Pages 2–3, 30–31 Shutterstock/Vincent St
Thomas; Page 5t Alamy/Chromomorange/Manfred Dietsch; 6–7 Alamy/Keasbury-Gordon
Photograph Collection; 7t Getty/Time Life Pictures; 8–9 Alamy/Classicstock; 8b Alamy/
Photos12 Collection; 9t Alamy/ArtArchive; 10b Getty/Heritage Images/Hulton Fine Art
Collection; 10–11 Alamy/B Lawrence; 12b, 25c Shutterstock/serjio74; 12–13 Flickr/Matt
Buck; 13t Getty/Central press/Hulton Archive; 14–15 Shutterstock/Aleksandr Riutin;
15t Flickr/Brandy; 15b Shutterstock/huyangshu; 16–17 Shutterstock/Viacheslav Lopatin;
16b Shutterstock/Manfred Steinbach; 17c Shutterstock/katatonia82; 18 Getty/SSPL/
Manchester Daily Express; 19 Flickr/Simon Pielow; 19t Getty/Gallo Images/Lanz von
Horsten; 20 Shutterstock/Matthew Siddons; 21t Shutterstock/trubityn; 21b Shutterstock/
antb; 22 Shutterstock/cyo bo; 23 Alamy/epa european pressphoto agency bv;
23t Shutterstock/ Leonid Andronov; 24 Getty/SSPL; 25 Flickr/News Oresund;
26 Shutterstock/Martin M303; 27t Alamy/AF Archive; 27b Shutterstock/Ron Ellis;
28 Flickr/scjody; 29 Shutterstock/Kijja Pruchyathamkorn; 29t Shutterstock/hanmon;
32 Dreamstime/Sébastien Bonaimé.

Front cover: The *Taroko Express*, a tilting express train, speeds through Taiwan.

CONTENTS

For your free audio download go to

http://panmacmillan.com/SpeedyTrains
or goo.gl/j0fqW1

Happy listening!

Scan me!

All kinds of train

A train is a vehicle that runs on rails. A train set is made up of a locomotive that pulls a number of carriages or cars. There are passenger trains, freight trains, luxury trains, underground trains— and toy trains!

FACT...

A wagonway was used in Greece in about 600 BCE to move boats across a small stretch of land.

Is it a boat? Is it a train? This train moves boats from one canal to another in Poland.

SPOTLIGHT: Bullet train O series

Famous for:	first high-speed train
Built for:	Tokaido–Shinkansen line, Japan
Built:	1964
Top speed:	130 mph (210km/h)

From cart to train

On 21 February, 1804, a steam
locomotive pulled a train along rails at
an ironworks in Wales. The railway age
had begun. Twenty years later,
George Stephenson opened
the first passenger railroad: the
Stockton and Darlington railway.

Locomotion No. 1 pulled the very first train
on the Stockton and Darlington Railway.
Its design helped to build future steam
locomotives, such as the *Rocket*.

Famous for:	ground-breaking steam locomotive
Designed by:	Robert Stephenson
Built:	1829
Top speed:	28 mph (45km/h)

FACT...

William Huskisson, the Member of Parliament for Liverpool, England, was hit and killed by the *Rocket* at the opening ceremony of the Liverpool and Manchester Railway in 1830.

The first passenger car looked like a road vehicle.

Railroads everywhere

Soon great projects built railroads across the world. Thousands and thousands of workers built the railroads by hand. It was dangerous and hard work.

Laborers working on the New York Central Railroad.

Three workers died for every mile of track built on the East African Railway.

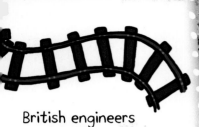

British engineers traveled around the world building railroads.

FACT...

In 1830, there were 98 miles (157 kilometers) of train track in Britain. By 1860 there were 10, 433 miles (16,790 kilometers).

The age of steam

Over the next 100 years, trains became the most popular form of long-distance transport for freight and passengers. Trains became faster and faster. In the 1930s, Sir Nigel Gresley built two record-breaking streamlined trains: the *Flying Scotsman* and *Mallard*.

Trains soon became the fastest way to travel long distances.

Famous for: fastest steam train
Designed by: Sir Nigel Gresley
Built: 1938
Top speed: 125 mph (201km/h)

Mallard is still the fastest-ever steam train.

MALLARD

Nº 446

Diesel, electric—and jet!

The first trains were steam trains— huge coal fires heated water to make steam to move the engine. Later, there were powerful diesel trains and fast electric trains. A few trains have even been built with jet engines.

FACT...

The first diesel engine was designed by Dr Rudolf Diesel.

Electric trains use electricity from overhead wires.

Turbo trains could travel at 155 miles
(250 kilometers) per hour.

Spotlight: Intercity 125

Famous for:	fastest diesel train in the world
Used by:	British Rail
First used:	1976
Top speed:	148 mph (238 km/h)

Great rail journeys

The first train journey was 25 miles (40 kilometers) long. Today, you can travel for thousands of miles across continents without changing trains. Passengers can eat in special dining carriages and can sleep in real beds.

The Trans-Siberian Railway travels across a third of the world in five-and-a-half days.

Russia–China: Moscow to Beijing
(Trans-Siberian Railway)   4862 mi. (7826km)
Canada: Toronto to Vancouver   2775 mi. (4466km)
Australia: Sydney to Perth   2704 mi. (4352km)
India: Dibrugarh to Kanyakumari 2633 mi. (4238km)

It takes three-and-a-half days to travel from Toronto to Vancouver in Canada.

It takes two days to travel from Shanghai (China) to Lhasa (Tibet, China).

Going underground

If you go to London, Paris, New York, or Shanghai there will be trains rumbling deep beneath your feet. There are 148 cities in the world with underground trains. The Shanghai Metro in China has the most track, the New York City Subway has the most stations and the Kiev Metro in the Ukraine is the deepest.

Komsomolskaya metro station in Moscow, Russia, looks like a palace.

Station in Munich, Germany

FACT...

Arsenalna Station on the Kiev Metro in the Ukraine is 344 feet (105 meters) below ground and is the deepest station in the world.

A tram is a small electric train that runs on rails in cities.

17

Luxury trains

Have you ever had to stand on a crowded train? Well, next time you travel, why don't you pick something more luxurious? Passengers can travel in style on the *Orient Express* across Europe, the *Blue Train* across South Africa, or the *Maharajas' Express* across India.

The *Orient Express*, the world's first luxury train, ran from Paris, France to Istanbul in Turkey.

FACT...

Suites onboard South Africa's *Blue Train* come with their own personal butler.

The *Blue Train*

The *Maharajas' Express* has two restaurants, a bar, a library, and a Presidential suite.

Working hard

Most of the world's goods are moved by train. Freight trains can have more than 600 goods wagons and be four miles (seven kilometers) long. Long goods trains sometimes have two or three locomotives pulling them.

Containers of goods can be double stacked on long trains.

Freight trains can move heavy items such as tankers or open wagons full of coal or rocks.

FACT...

A fully laden freight train can take over half a mile (one kilometer) to stop.

A snow blower is used to clear snowy tracks in Canada.

Fastest trains

High-speed trains travel at top speeds on special electric lines. The trains have sleek shapes to cut throug the air. The fastest trains today are held four inches (10 centimeters) above the rails by magnets.

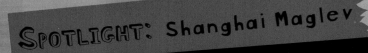

SPOTLIGHT: Shanghai Maglev

Famous for:	fastest scheduled train
First used:	2004
Average speed:	155 mph (251km/h)
Top speed:	267 mph (430km/h)

The TGV is France's high-speed train.

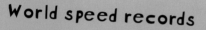

World speed records

Conventional train in test: TGV—357 mph (575km/h (2007)

Non-conventional train in test:
LO Series Maglev—375 mph (603km/h) (2015)

Scheduled train: Shanghai Maglev—367 mph (430km/h)

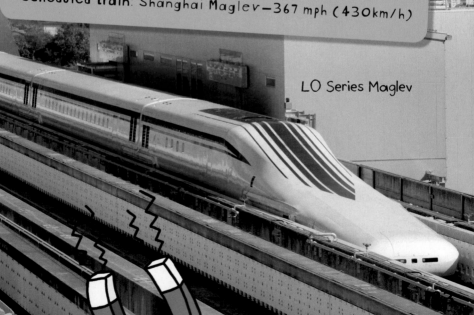

LO Series Maglev

Tunnels and bridges

Trains are not very good at going up or down steep hills. Bridges and tunnels are built to help keep the track flat and to cross rivers and roads.

Enormous tunnel-boring machines were used to dig the 31-mile-long (50-kilometer-long) Channel Tunnel.

FACT...

The longest rail bridge in the world is the Danyang-Kunshun Bridge in China. It is 103 miles (165 kilometers) long and took 10,000 people four years to build.

The Landwasser viaduct in Switzerland goes into a tunnel in the cliff face.

The bridge and tunnel that connect Sweden and Denmark meet at an artificial island.

Trains in movies

Some of the most famous trains of all time only exist in books and movies: the *Hogwarts Express*, Thomas the Tank Engine, and the *Polar Express*.

The *Hogwarts Express* crossed the Glenfinnan viaduct in Scotland.

The *Polar Express* took children to see Santa Claus.

FACT...

Reverend Wilbert Awdry created the story of Thomas the Tank Engine to cheer up his son Christopher while he had measles.

Unlike the other engines, Thomas carries his own water (in a tank) and coal.

Highest, longest, cutest

Every day 20 million people travel on Indian railroads. Here are some more amazing train numbers.

Longest railway: Moscow to Vladivostock 5771 miles (9259 kilometers)

Highest railway: Tanggula Pass, Tibet, China 16,640 feet (5072 meters)

Longest passenger train: Ringling Bros. and Barnum & Bailey Circus trains—1 mile (1.6km)

Busiest train station: Shinjuko Station, Tokyo, Japan—1.26 million passengers a day

The cutest train? Japanese train *Tama Densha* is covered in pictures of the railroad cat.

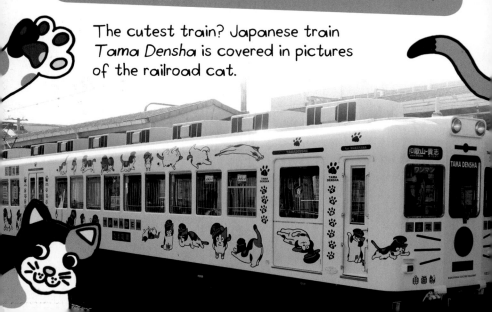

The Gornergrat Rack Railway in Switzerland is the highest open-air railway in Europe.

When there is no room inside the train, people are allowed to travel on the roof in India.

वातानुकूलित 2-टियर शयनयान
AC TWO TIER SLEEPER

आपातकालीन खिड़की

GLOSSARY

bullet train The nickname of the *Shinkansen*, a high-speed passenger train in Japan.

butler A servant that looks after you.

canal A river that has been built by people. Boats can travel along it.

container A large metal box that you can put things into.

diesel train A train with an engine that runs on diesel fuel.

electric train A train that runs on electricity from overhead cables or live rails.

freight train A train that carries materials, heavy loads and other things, but not passengers.

high-speed train A fast train that runs on its own special track.

ironworks A place where iron is made.

locomotive A railroad engine that pulls railroad wagons.

luxury train A train with the most comfortable carriages.

Maglev A train that is held above the rails by magnets.

snow blower A train that clears snow off rail tracks.

steam train A train that uses steam to move.

suite A group of rooms.

turbo train A train that is powered by a jet engine.

underground train A train that runs through tunnels underneath big cities.

viaduct A bridge over a valley.

wagonway A simple railroad track for wagons.

INDEX